THE MANUFACTURED ARAB

The Story of How Hollywood's False Storytelling Shaped Public Acceptance of Human Suffering

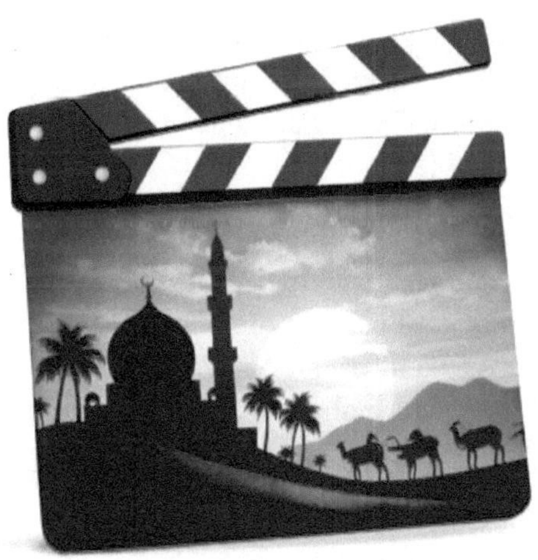

DR. ABRAHAM KHOUREIS, Ph.D.

Author of HOLLYWOOD DREAM

A Hollywood Talent Agent

Copyright Notice

ANG POWER PUBLISHING HOUSE
PO BOX 10735 / Glendale, CA 91209-USA
ANGPowerPHouse@Gmail.com
ISBN: 978-1-966837-48-0

Printed in the United States of America

Note & Disclaimer

This book is a work of literature inspired by true events. While it draws from historical accounts, traditions, and collective memory, certain characters, dialogues, and scenes have been adapted for narrative purposes. Although it is based on accurate historical resources, it is not intended to serve as a definitive historical record.

Any resemblance to actual persons, living or deceased, as well as to organizations, institutions, governments, or groups, beyond the well-known historical figures and entities referenced, is entirely coincidental and unintentional.

The purpose of this work is to honor the essence of events and to explore their moral, spiritual, and human significance through the medium of authentic and real storytelling.

“Hollywood has a quiet power, it decides who is complex and who is convenient. For Arabs and Muslims, the role was written long before the camera rolled.”

Dr. Abraham Khoureis

A Note to the Reader

Much of what the world has been shown about Arabs and Muslims through popular films and media is false.

This does not mean every story was invented out of malice, but it does mean that over time, Hollywood and major media repeatedly presented a narrow and distorted image that does not reflect real people, real societies, or real history. Arabs were often portrayed as violent, irrational, or backward. Muslims were framed almost exclusively through fear. Palestinians were frequently erased altogether or reduced to nameless figures without voice or dignity.

What makes these portrayals especially dishonest is that they erase a long and well-documented truth.

Arab and Muslim civilizations were central to the development of the modern world. They preserved and expanded human knowledge at times when Europe was struggling to do so. Algebra, algorithms, and foundational mathematics were developed and refined by Arab and Muslim scholars. Advances in medicine, surgery, pharmacology, and hospitals came from the Muslim world and were studied in Europe for centuries.

Astronomy, optics, chemistry, navigation, architecture, and engineering were all shaped by Arab and Muslim thinkers whose work later became the backbone of Western education.

Even the Renaissance did not arise in isolation. Europe relied heavily on Arab and Muslim scholarship, translated from Arabic into Latin, to recover the works of Aristotle, Plato, Galen, and others. Universities across Europe taught from texts written or preserved by Arab and Muslim scholars for generations. Over time, these contributions were pushed aside, forgotten, or deliberately minimized.

As Arabs and Muslims came to be portrayed as threats rather than contributors, their role in human progress was quietly dismissed. The image of the Arab as backward replaced the reality of the Arab as educator. The image of the Muslim as dangerous replaced the truth of the Muslim as physician, mathematician, philosopher, and builder of institutions.

This shift did not happen naturally. It happened through malicious repetition. Through selective false storytelling. Through intentional framing that disconnected a people from their history and their humanity.

In this book, I explore how that good image of the God-fearing and civilizations building Arabs and Muslims was falsely manufactured; how it was repeated until it felt normal, and how it helped justify fear, exclusion, and violence. It also asks what was lost when truth was replaced by convenience, and how much damage can be done when entire civilizations are reduced or its contributions dismissed.

The Manufactured Arab is about accuracy. About restoring context. And about recognizing that when history is erased long enough, the present becomes easier to manipulate.

“Most people have never truly met an Arab or a Muslim, only the version manufactured about them. When they finally meet the human being behind the narrative, the story unravels, leaving dignity, faith, and a shared humanity.”

Dr. Abraham Khoureis

Table of Contents

Author's Note

While scholars have documented Hollywood's systematic stereotyping and the media's role in shaping public perception of Arabs and Muslims, this book names that process directly.
I call it, *The Manufactured Arab*."

Preface

I am writing this book as someone who works inside Hollywood, not as an outsider guessing how it functions. I am a talent agent. I am the author of Hollywood Dream: How to Make It in Tinseltown. I understand how stories are pitched, approved, softened, sharpened, or buried. I understand how "creative choices" are often business choices, and how business choices are often political, even when no one wants to say that word out loud.

This idea for this book began with a moment of honesty that I did not expect.

I was in a professional meeting with senior people in the industry, including a studio executive with real power, not a minor figure, not someone speaking hypothetically. During the conversation, he spoke openly about Gaza, and he did not use vague language. He said plainly that what was happening was morally wrong. He did not sound defensive. He sounded troubled.

Then he said something that stopped the room.

He acknowledged that for decades, the intentional portrayal of Arabs and Muslims in Hollywood films and television had been morally corrupt. Those were his words in substance, if not rehearsed phrasing. He said that Arabs and Muslims were deliberately shown in negative ways, not by accident, not because of ignorance, but because those portrayals served a purpose. They helped justify what was happening to Palestinians on the ground. They made it easier for audiences to accept occupation, violence, and dispossession.

He went further. He said we should not do this anymore.

To me, that mattered. Why?

Because this was not said by an activist. It was not said by someone trying to make a public statement. It was said by a studio head speaking honestly in a room where he assumed people understood the mechanics of power and storytelling.

He did not deny responsibility. He named it. He said that what the industry had done was wrong, and that continuing it would also be wrong.

No one laughed. No one challenged him. No one accused him of exaggeration. The room was quiet, not because people disagreed, but because what he said fit too well with what many of us had already seen.

As a Hollywood insider, I can say this plainly. Stories are not neutral. Repetition is not accidental. When the same group of people is shown again and again as violent, irrational, or disposable, the audience learns something whether they intend to or not. When Arabs are rarely shown as families living ordinary lives, their suffering becomes easier to explain away. When land is taken, it sounds like security. When people are killed, it sounds like defense.

This did not happen once. It happened over decades.

Hollywood helped shape an emotional environment where Americans could hear about Palestinian homes being destroyed and Palestinian children being killed without feeling the urgency they would feel if the same thing were happening to people they recognized as familiar. That is not a small failure. That is a moral failure.

I am not writing this book because I am part of this industry, and silence would make me complicit. When someone with power inside the system openly admits that what we have done was morally corrupt, and that we should stop doing it, that moment deserves to be recorded.

This book is not a call for censorship. It is a call for honesty. Arabs and Palestinians are not characters designed to make other people's stories easier. They are human beings with lives, families, history, humor, fear, and love. When we remove that humanity on screen, we help remove it in real life.

I am letting the chips fall where they may because this is

bigger than careers or comfort. The occupation of Palestinian land did not happen in a vacuum. It was supported by stories that made it tolerable. If that truth is uncomfortable, it should be. Moral clarity usually is.

I am writing as Dr. Abe, a Hollywood talent agent and insider, because this conversation should not only come from those who are harmed, but also from those who helped shape the system, even indirectly. The industry has power. With that power comes responsibility.

This book exists because someone inside the system finally said out loud what many had practiced for decades, that the portrayal of Arabs and Palestinians was intentional, wrong, and must stop. Once that is said, there is no honest way to look away.

Dr. Abe

Introduction

This book is about how a people were shown to the public, again and again, in ways that made harm and cruelty against them easier to accept.

For decades, Arabs and Muslims appeared in American movies and television in a limited and damaging set of roles. They were commonly portrayed as terrorists, extremists, hijackers, oil sheik villains, fanatics driven by religion, or angry men shouting in broken English. They were rarely shown as teachers, doctors, shop owners, parents, or neighbors. They were rarely shown living normal lives. When violence happened to them, the story did not pause. Their deaths were not treated as losses. They were treated as solutions.

These portrayals were not subtle. They followed clear patterns that can be traced across time.

Beginning in early Hollywood and accelerating after the mid-twentieth century, Arab characters were often introduced as threats to Western safety or stability. In action films and political thrillers, Arabs were framed as faceless enemies whose motives did not require explanation. In dramas, they were depicted as backward, irrational, or cruel. In comedies, they were reduced to caricatures. In many cases, they did not even have names. They existed to be feared, defeated, or removed so the story could move forward.

Muslims, in particular, were frequently portrayed as driven entirely by religion, as if belief itself made them violent or incapable of reason. This framing suggested that conflict with them was inevitable and that force was the only possible response. When a group is shown this way repeatedly, the audience learns to expect violence from them and to accept violence against them.

Palestinians were treated even more invisibly.

They were rarely shown as people living on a land with history, villages, farms, and families. Palestine was not presented as a place where ordinary life existed. It was presented as a conflict zone, a security problem, a backdrop for someone else's story. When Palestinians appeared, they were often unnamed, shown briefly, and removed quickly. Their suffering was compressed into seconds and then replaced by the next plot point.

This pattern did not come from a single film or a single studio. It was built over time, through repetition. Scholars, journalists, and media watchdog groups have documented these portrayals for decades. The record exists. The patterns are visible. They are not imagined.

This mattered because while these images were shaping public perception, and opinion, something very real was happening in the world.

Palestinian land was being taken. Homes were being destroyed. Families were being displaced. People were being killed. This happened gradually, over many years. For much of the American public, these cruel inhumane events did not register as an ongoing moral emergency. They registered as part of a complicated situation, something distant, something already explained.

That response did not come from studying authentic history. It came from years of exposure to the same negative images.

When a people are consistently shown as violent, unstable, or less than fully human, their suffering becomes easier to justify. Land theft starts to sound like security. Killing starts to sound like defense. Silence starts to feel reasonable.

This is where storytelling matters.

Hollywood has been one of the most powerful forces shaping emotional instinct in American life. People learn who to trust, who to fear, and who to ignore not from policy papers, but from repeated images. Movies and television teach viewers what feels normal and what feels threatening. They teach when to pause and feel, and when to move on without asking questions.

Over many decades, Arabs and Muslims, including Palestinians, were repeatedly portrayed in narrow and negative ways. These portrayals did not always scream hostility. Often, they were quiet, routine, and forgettable. But repetition gives weight to even subtle messages. When the same group is shown over and over as a problem, a threat, or a background presence without depth, viewers begin to absorb that framing without realizing it.

This book explores how these negative portrayals helped make the occupation of Palestinian land emotionally acceptable to American audiences. Not by telling people to approve of it, but by shaping how they understood the people it was happening to. When Palestinians appear mainly as faceless figures connected to danger, their suffering does not demand the same response as suffering that feels close and recognizable.

Hollywood was not the only force shaping this perception, but it was a powerful one. Movies and television trained emotional reflexes. Later, news outlets and media commentary often reinforced the same framing, using language that repeated what audiences already recognized. The point here is simpler. The groundwork was laid through intentionally false storytelling long before headlines appeared.

This book does not claim that every filmmaker, journalist, or executive acted with the same intent. It does claim that a consistent portrayal served a political reality. The repeated image of the Arab and the Muslim as a threat made it easier for Americans to accept what was happening to Palestinians without sustained outrage or resistance.

As someone who works inside Hollywood, I am writing from experience and from what was finally admitted openly by someone with real power in the industry. The portrayal was intentional. It was wrong. It was immoral. And it helped make injustice easier to tolerate.

Here, I am not asking the reader to take sides. I am asking the reader to look carefully at the story they have been told for most of their lives and to consider what that story made possible. This book is about connecting image to outcome, storytelling to policy, and perception to permission.

If Palestinians had been widely seen as ordinary people living ordinary lives on a lived-in land, what has happened to them would have been far harder to justify or ignore. That is the question this book keeps returning to. To make visible what was hidden in plain sight.

Once these connections are seen clearly, it becomes harder to dismiss what has happened as accidental or unavoidable.

That is where the story of the manufactured Arab begins.

"Hollywood has a lot of influence, it decides who gets depth and who gets reduced to a stereotype. For Arabs the role was decided long ago."

Dr. Abe Khoureis

Chapter 1

Let's Begin

What followed that moment in the room was not resolution. There was no collective reckoning, no sudden collapse of the old order. People stood, gathered their things, spoke politely, and returned to their lives. That, too, is part of the truth. Systems do not unravel because a truth is spoken aloud once. They endure because most people learn how to carry what they know without letting it disrupt their position within the system.

I carried it differently.

Once something like that is said plainly, by someone who has no reason to perform or exaggerate, it changes how memory organizes itself. Scenes from films once watched casually begin to rearrange. Lines of dialogue replay themselves with new weight. Characters that once felt incidental now appear purposeful. The absence of humanity where it should have been becomes impossible to unsee.

What had always been explained away as coincidence or market demand now revealed a pattern. Not a conspiracy whispered in shadows, but a professional logic discussed openly among people who understood narrative as leverage. Stories were not merely entertainment. They were preparation. They trained emotional reflexes. They taught audiences who deserved patience and who did not, whose pain required context and whose pain could be summarized.

This realization brings with it an uncomfortable responsibility. Not just for those who built the stories, but for those who benefited from them, repeated them, funded them, distributed them, and consumed them without question. Responsibility does not mean guilt. It means awareness followed by choice. It means recognizing that neutrality is rarely neutral when power and suffering are unevenly distributed.

For Arab Americans, this awareness has long been lived rather than discovered. Watching oneself slowly disappear from the screen as a full human being creates a particular kind of fracture. It teaches you to explain yourself before you are asked, to soften your language, to carry an invisible burden of reassurance. It teaches children that they must be exceptional simply to be seen as ordinary. It teaches parents to fear how their children will be perceived long before they fear how they will be treated.

The cost of this conditioning is not abstract. It shows up in policy debates stripped of empathy, in headlines that read like procedures rather than tragedies, in public conversations where some lives are discussed with care and others with calculation. When a people have already been flattened in the imagination, their suffering arrives pre-rationalized.

This is why testimony matters.

Not because it changes everything at once, but because it interrupts the story that claims there is nothing to question. A single moment of honesty, spoken inside the machinery itself, exposes the distance between what is shown and what is known. It reminds us that narratives are made, not inevitable, and that what has been constructed can be dismantled.

I am not going to ask you as a reader to abandon critical thought. I am asking you to pay attention for memory, for the courage to sit with discomfort rather than dismiss it. I ask you to notice what happens when we look back at the stories we were told and ask not whether they were compelling, but whether they were fair, whether they were complete, whether they allowed a people to remain human.

The manufactured image of an Arab did not arise because Arabs lacked humanity. On the contrary, they are ones of the most compassionate people you can meet. It arose because humanity complicated a political project that required silence more than understanding. Once that is acknowledged, the question is no longer whether storytelling became a weapon. It is whether we are willing to disarm it. And that decision, unlike the stories we inherited, is still ours to make.

Chapter 2

When Stories Prepare the Ground

I had been in this room many times before, orderly, restrained, populated by people who understand how to speak without revealing too much and how to listen without reacting. Directors, producers, talent, executives, people whose careers depend on shaping narratives while appearing detached from them. A professional meeting among peers. Familiar faces. Familiar cadence. An unspoken understanding that what is said here stays here.

Then one executive spoke in a way that broke the pattern.

He was not polished. He was not guarded. He spoke as someone personally unsettled. Affected. The word he used entered the room without preparation or framing. Genocide. Gaza. Not as rhetoric. Not as provocation. Simply as recognition. As something that had pierced the professional armor and demanded to be named plainly.

As the conversation continued, it shifted inward. Away from headlines and outward conflict, toward the industry itself. Toward history. Toward intention. It was the kind of turn that rarely happens in public but occasionally surfaces in rooms where people assume shared understanding. Someone asked a question directly, “Are you sure the negative portrayal of Arabs in Hollywood was planned? Was it intentional?

The answer came without hesitation.

Yes.

No pause. No qualifiers. No attempt to dilute the earlier admission. It was not offered defensively, nor wrapped in ideology. It was stated as fact, as a professional acknowledgment of how things had been done in Hollywood, and why.

He explained that Arabs and Muslims had been portrayed consistently in ways that made them easier to fear and harder to empathize with. Not because writers lacked imagination, and not because audiences demanded it, but because perception mattered. Because perception protected outcomes. Because if Arabs were seen fully as human, the project unfolding on Palestinian land would become emotionally difficult to sustain for the American public.

As villages were taken, destroyed and renamed, one by one, he said, American support needed to remain stable. That stability could not survive widespread empathy. It required distance. It required a story in which Palestinians were not fully visible as people whose lives carried equal weight.

No one interrupted him.

The silence that followed was not shock. It was recognition. The kind that settles in a room when something long understood privately is finally spoken aloud. No one challenged the logic. No one argued the premise. It did not feel like scandal. It felt like disclosure.

What stayed with me was not only what was said, but the manner in which it was said. Calmly. Matter of fact. Without urgency. Without shame. As if this were not a moral rupture, but a strategic explanation shared among professionals fluent in the language of narrative utility.

In that moment, decades of film and television rearranged themselves in my mind. Scenes I had once watched casually now appeared purposeful. Characters that once seemed incidental revealed a pattern. The absence of humanity where it should have been was no longer subtle. It was deliberate.

I left that meeting with a clarity that has not faded. Not the clarity of outrage, but the clarity of confirmation. The understanding that what Palestinians experienced on the ground was mirrored by what Arabs and Muslims experienced on screen. One enabled the other. One softened resistance to the other.

He wasn't telling us about a theory. It is not conjecture. He was providing a conscious testimony.

The process, however, did not begin with villains or declarations. There was no announcement. No memo. No public moment instructing America to see a people differently. That is not how perception changes. It moves quietly. Gradually. So gently that by the time it is noticed, it already feels normal.

At first, the Arab simply drifted away from the center of the story. From protagonist to background. From neighbor to foreign presence. The warmth did not vanish suddenly. It thinned. It cooled. It became conditional. Then the tone hardened. A line of dialogue carried suspicion. An accent signaled danger before a word was spoken. A character appeared only to be removed so the story could proceed.

The Arab was no longer written to live a life. He was written to serve a function.

Fear does not need to be declared to be learned. It only requires repetition. Over time, repetition did its work. Arab characters lost interior lives. They were rarely shown loving their children, grieving losses, or existing without menace. Motivation was simplified. Emotion flattened. Humanity quietly erased. Names became unnecessary. The role alone was sufficient.

The audience adjusted, not out of cruelty, but out of conditioning. Stories teach us how to see. They teach us whose pain requires explanation and whose does not, whose suffering interrupts the narrative and whose advances it. Once the Arab was no longer portrayed as fully human, violence against him no longer disrupted the story. It belonged within it.

This is where storytelling shifts from reflection to conditioning. When a people are seen only through suspicion, compassion begins to feel misplaced. Questions seem excessive. Silence starts to feel reasonable. By the time distant villages disappeared, the emotional groundwork had already been laid. The public did not need persuasion. They had been prepared.

This is not an accusation of the audience. It is an observation about influence. People absorb what they are shown repeatedly, especially when it comes through familiar formats, trusted studios, and voices they have been trained to believe. When the same industry that once offered wonder begins offering inevitability, the transition feels earned rather than imposed.

Hollywood storytelling did not simply reflect political reality. It helped construct the emotional conditions that allowed occupation to continue without sustained moral interruption. It trained viewers not to ask who was losing their home, but who was causing problems. Not whose land was taken, but why security required it.

Once that framing settled in, Palestinian suffering no longer disrupted the narrative.

That is how an image becomes a weapon. Not by demanding hatred, but by removing hesitation. Not by calling for violence, but by making violence feel already justified.

Once you see that process from the inside, you cannot return to the comfort of believing it was accidental.

This book exists because what was said in that room deserves to be preserved. Not to expose individuals, but to expose a mechanism. Because land was not taken by force alone. It was taken through stories. And those stories had done their work long before the world recognized what they were designed to make acceptable.

Chapter 3

How the Image Was Built on Screen

To understand how this happened, you have to start with what people actually saw.

For decades, when Arabs and Muslims appeared in American movies and television, they were usually shown in a very narrow set of ways. The most common roles were terrorists, hijackers, extremists, angry mobs, oil-rich villains, religious fanatics, or violent men shouting slogans. These characters were often unnamed, interchangeable, and disposable. They were not written as individuals with personal lives. They existed to create fear or justify action by the hero.

If an Arab character appeared in an action film, the audience could usually predict what would happen to him. He would be the enemy. He would be aggressive. He would likely die, and when he did, the story would not slow down. There would be no pause to show who he was, who loved him, or what was lost. His death would move the plot forward.

This pattern did not come from one studio or one decade. It repeated itself across generations of films. Early portrayals leaned heavily on caricature, Arabs as backward, cruel, or exotic threats. As time went on, the imagery modernized, but the message stayed the same. The Arab became the terrorist. The Muslim became the extremist. The accent became a warning sign. The setting became chaotic and dangerous by default.

Palestinians were almost entirely missing as people.

When Palestine appeared on screen, it was rarely shown as a place where ordinary life existed. You did not see families eating dinner, children walking to school, farmers tending land, shopkeepers opening stores. Instead, Palestine was treated as a trouble spot, a background location where violence was expected. Palestinians, when shown at all, were often reduced to crowds, silhouettes, or brief images connected to unrest.

This mattered because audiences learn what feels normal from what they see repeatedly. When a group of people is never shown living ordinary lives, the audience does not learn to recognize them as neighbors or equals. They learn to see them as a problem.

Hollywood often defends these portrayals by saying they reflect reality. But that explanation falls apart when the same reality is shown only one way. Every society has ordinary people and extremists. Every land has daily life and conflict. But Hollywood did not balance these images when it came to Arabs and Muslims. It overwhelmingly showed one side and ignored the other.

Over time, this built a mental shortcut for viewers. Arab meant danger. Muslim meant threat. Palestinian meant trouble. These associations did not require conscious agreement. They became automatic.

What made this especially powerful is that these portrayals were not framed as political statements. They were framed as entertainment. Viewers were not told they were being taught anything. They were just watching stories. That is why the impact lasted.

By the time news coverage showed real Palestinians being displaced or killed, many viewers already had a frame in place. They had seen similar images before. The people on the screen already fit a role they recognized. The story felt familiar, even when the suffering was real.

This is how storytelling shapes tolerance.

Hollywood did not need to tell audiences to support occupation. It only needed to remove the human connection that would make occupation feel unacceptable. When Arabs and Palestinians are shown mainly as threats or faceless figures, their loss does not register as a moral crisis. It registers as part of an ongoing problem.

Here, I am not suggesting that every filmmaker intended harm. It is showing that the result was harm, sustained over decades, through consistent choices. When the same type of portrayal repeats long enough, it stops being coincidence. It becomes a system.

That system shaped how Americans saw Arabs and Muslims long before they ever heard the word Gaza on the news. And once that image was set, it became much easier for real-world violence and dispossession to be accepted without serious challenge. That is how the image was built.

Chapter 4

From Repetition to Acceptance

What turned these portrayals into something powerful was not shock. It was repetition.

People did not see one movie and walk away with a fixed opinion about Arabs or Muslims. They saw the same types of characters over and over again, across different stories, different years, different platforms. Each appearance reinforced the last. Over time, those portrayals stopped feeling like choices and started feeling like reality.

When the same group of people is shown repeatedly as violent, unstable, or threatening, the viewer does not have to consciously agree with the message for it to stick. The brain fills in gaps automatically. The viewer begins to expect certain behavior before it happens. An accent becomes a warning. A face becomes a signal. The story no longer needs explanation because the audience already "knows" who this person is supposed to be.

This process is quiet. It does not feel like influence. It feels like familiarity.

Hollywood did not need to exaggerate endlessly. It only needed to stay consistent. The Arab or Muslim character rarely appeared as a normal person living a normal life. He did not go to work, worry about bills, argue with family, or plan for the future. He existed mainly at moments of tension or violence. When he disappeared, the story moved on without asking the audience to feel loss.

This taught viewers something important, even if they never put it into words. It taught them that Arab and Muslim lives were not meant to be followed closely. They were not meant to be remembered. They were part of the environment, not the heart of the story.

As this pattern repeated, it shaped expectations outside of entertainment.

When real events involving Arabs or Muslims appeared on the news, viewers did not approach them with fresh eyes. They brought expectations with them. Violence felt unsurprising. Suffering felt distant. Explanations felt unnecessary. The situation already fit a familiar story.

This is where acceptance begins.

Acceptance does not mean approval. It means a lack of urgency. It means hearing about harm and assuming it must be part of something complicated, something unavoidable, something already handled by people in charge. The viewer does not feel the need to stop, question, or demand accountability.

For Palestinians, this had serious consequences.

As land was taken, homes destroyed, and lives lost, many Americans processed the information through the same frame they had learned from entertainment. Palestinians were not widely seen as families losing everything. They were seen as part of a conflict that never seemed to change. Their suffering blended into a pattern the audience had already accepted.

This did not require people to abandon their values. It required only that those values were never fully activated. Compassion depends on recognition. Recognition depends on familiarity. When familiarity is built around threat instead of humanity, compassion struggles to take hold.

The repetition of these portrayals did not create outrage fatigue. It created moral numbness. Events that should have triggered alarm instead triggered resignation. People did not say, "This is right." They said, "This is how it is."

That is the power of repetition. It does not persuade loudly. It conditions quietly. It reshapes instinct so that when injustice appears, it does not feel new or shocking enough to disrupt routine.

By the time occupation required ongoing political support, the emotional groundwork had already been laid. The audience did not need to be convinced again and again. They had already learned how to receive the story.

In this chapter, together, we explored and inquired about understanding how acceptance forms. When the same image is repeated for long enough, it stops being questioned. It becomes background. And background is where the most powerful influence often lives. That is how repetition turned portrayal into acceptance.

Chapter 5

Palestine Without People

One of the most important parts of this story is not what was shown, but what was missing.

When Americans saw stories connected to Palestine, they rarely saw Palestine as a place where ordinary life existed. They did not see towns waking up in the morning, shops opening, kids going to school, farmers working their land, or families gathering at night. Those details matter because they are what make a place feel real and human.

Instead, Palestine was usually presented as a problem area. A conflict zone. A security concern. A place where violence was expected and where normal life was assumed not to exist. When Palestinians appeared on screen, they were often shown in moments of unrest, shouting crowds, masked figures, brief flashes of anger or chaos. They were rarely introduced as individuals with names, histories, or futures.

This absence shaped perception more than any explicit message could have.

When a people are not shown living ordinary lives, it becomes harder for viewers to imagine what is being taken from them. A demolished home is no longer a family losing shelter, memories, and stability. It becomes footage of an event. A death is no longer a person whose life mattered to others. It becomes a statistic.

Hollywood did not show Palestinian villages before they were destroyed. It did not show families tending land passed down through generations. It did not show children growing up in neighborhoods that had meaning and history. Without those images, the audience had nothing to attach their empathy to.

This mattered deeply when real events unfolded.

When viewers heard that homes were being destroyed or land was being taken, the information did not collide with a clear mental picture of what that meant for real people. There was no sense of what daily life looked like before the loss. Without that contrast, dispossession sounded abstract. It sounded like policy rather than devastation.

Even when Palestinians appeared briefly in news coverage, the framing often matched what entertainment had already taught. They were shown at moments of conflict, not moments of living. Their grief was rarely followed over time. Their losses were not tracked. The story moved on.

By comparison, Israeli life was often shown in detail. Viewers saw families, children, routines, and fears. That difference mattered. One side was familiar. The other was distant. One side felt real. The other felt symbolic.

This imbalance did not require anyone to say that Palestinian lives mattered less. It communicated that idea without words.

When a people are rarely shown living, their deaths do not interrupt the story in the same way. The audience does not feel the same shock or urgency because the human connection was never fully formed. Without that connection, outrage struggles to take hold.

This is how Palestine was slowly emptied of people in the public imagination.

It was not erased completely. It was flattened. Reduced to a setting rather than a society. Reduced to a conflict rather than a community. Reduced to something that could be discussed without naming what was being lost.

Once that happens, occupation becomes easier to explain. Violence becomes easier to justify. Silence becomes easier to maintain.

In this chapter I am not suggesting that filmmakers sat down to erase Palestinian life intentionally in every case. It is showing that the result was the same. A people were made invisible where visibility mattered most.

And when people are invisible, what happens to them can continue for a long time without forcing the world to stop and look. That absence set the stage for everything that followed.

Chapter 6

When the News Picked Up the Same Story

By the time the news became the main source of information about Palestine for many Americans, the basic frame was already familiar. People had seen it for years in movies and television. The news did not start the story. It continued it.

This matters because news is supposed to slow things down and clarify what is happening. Instead, much of the reporting followed the same patterns people already recognized. The language sounded official and neutral, but the effect was not neutral.

When Palestinians were killed, headlines often used passive language. Words like "clashes," "crossfire," or "violence erupted" appeared again and again. These phrases made it unclear who did what to whom. Death sounded like an accident of chaos rather than the result of force. When Israeli actions were described, they were often framed as responses, retaliation, or security measures. That framing suggested necessity before facts were even presented.

Over time, readers learned how to read between the lines.

When Israeli civilians were harmed, stories often included names, ages, family details, and extended coverage. When Palestinian civilians were harmed, coverage was frequently brief. Numbers were given, but faces were not followed. Stories moved on quickly. There was rarely continuity. One incident did not connect to the next in a way that showed an ongoing pattern of loss.

This difference shaped perception.

It taught audiences whose lives required explanation and whose deaths could be summarized. It taught which suffering deserved depth and which suffering could be processed as background information. Again, this did not require hostility. It required habit.

The same thing happened with land.

When Palestinian land was taken or homes were demolished, reporting often focused on the reason given rather than the impact. Security concerns were emphasized. Legal language was used. The human cost was mentioned briefly, if at all. Readers were told why something happened before they were shown what it did to people.

That order matters.

When explanation comes before human detail, the mind settles into acceptance. The reader assumes there must be justification. The emotional question, "What would this feel like if it happened to me?" never fully forms.

This pattern repeated across major news outlets. Not in exactly the same way, but often enough to reinforce a single understanding. Palestinians appeared mainly at moments of unrest. Their lives outside of conflict remained largely unseen. Their losses were rarely tracked over time in a way that showed accumulation.

The news did not have to persuade audiences that 77 years occupation was good. It only needed to present it as normal, ongoing, and complicated. When something is framed as complicated for long enough, people stop asking moral questions. They assume someone else is handling it.

This is where the media machine quietly aligned with what entertainment had already taught.

Hollywood ***shaped*** expectation. News outlets ***reinforced*** it. One provided the emotional frame. The other provided the daily confirmation. Together, they created a closed loop. Arabs and Palestinians appeared as problems. Israeli actions appeared as responses. The imbalance felt natural because it had been learned.

This does not mean every journalist intended harm. Newsrooms are complex. Pressure is constant. Sources matter. Language gets recycled. But systems can produce outcomes even without shared intent. When the same framing repeats across time and platforms, the result is consistent whether planned or not.

The outcome was clear.

American audiences were rarely invited to sit with Palestinian suffering long enough to feel its weight. The story moved too quickly. The language softened the impact. The framing suggested inevitability.

That is how silence holds.

By the time violence escalated again and again, outrage struggled to take root. Not because people approved, but because the story never stopped long enough to demand a response. The machinery kept moving.

In this chapter, together, we recognize how language and repetition shape public understanding. When news adopts the same assumptions as entertainment, it stops correcting the story and starts reinforcing it. That is how perception becomes policy-friendly.

That is how occupation stays tolerable. And once that alignment is recognized, it cannot be unseen.

Chapter 7

How Hollywood Packages a People

Hollywood does not operate randomly. Nothing that appears on screen repeatedly for decades does. Characters are not accidents. Images are not coincidences. What audiences see again and again is usually the result of choices, approvals, and incentives.

Inside the industry, this is called packaging.

Packaging means deciding in advance how something will be presented so it can be easily understood, marketed, and consumed. Studios package genres, heroes, villains, cultures, even accents. They decide what signals danger, what signals trust, and what signals familiarity. Once a package works, it is reused.

That is exactly what happened with Arabs and Muslims.

Hollywood packaged "the Arab" as a type. Not as an individual, not as a range of people, but as a recognizable product. Audiences learned quickly what this package meant. Certain looks, certain accents, certain locations, certain behaviors. You did not need backstory. You did not need explanation. The package did the work.

From an industry perspective, this was efficient.

When writers pitched stories, they did not need to explain who the antagonist was if he fit the package. Executives understood it immediately. Casting followed the same logic. Directors knew how to shoot it. Editors knew how long to linger. Music cues reinforced the message. Everything worked together to deliver the same result.

This is how stereotypes become systems.

Once the Arab was packaged as a threat, it became risky to show something different. Complexity slows pacing. Humanity complicates plots. A fully developed Arab character requires time, context, and care. Studios are often unwilling to invest that effort when a simpler package already delivers the desired reaction.

So the package stayed.

Arab characters were rarely allowed to exist outside moments of danger. They were rarely shown as professionals, parents, neighbors, or people with inner lives. When they appeared, they appeared to serve a purpose in someone else's story. Once that purpose was fulfilled, they disappeared.

Palestinians, when included at all, were folded into this same package or removed entirely. They were not marketed as people whose stories could stand on their own. They were treated as part of the same background noise, interchangeable, replaceable, expendable.

From a business standpoint, this made sense inside Hollywood logic. The package had already been accepted by audiences. It did not create confusion. It did not require explanation. It did not threaten box office returns.

From a moral standpoint, it was devastating.

Packaging strips people of individuality. It reduces entire communities to a handful of traits. It makes harm easier to justify because the audience is not responding to a person. They are responding to a product they have been trained to recognize.

As a Hollywood insider, I can say this clearly. When something is packaged and repeated long enough, it stops being questioned inside the system. It becomes "what works." New writers inherit it. New executives approve it. No one feels responsible because no one feels like they created it.

That is how moral failure spreads without a single villain.

This packaging also shaped what stories were never told. Scripts that showed Arabs or Muslims living normal lives struggled to move forward. Stories that centered Arab humanity were often labeled risky, political, or niche. Meanwhile, stories that reinforced the existing package were considered safe.

The result was predictable. Audiences were rarely given a chance to see Arabs outside the manufactured image. And when you are never shown something, you are less likely to imagine it on your own.

In this chapter, together, we explored industry habit that had real consequences. When Hollywood packaged the Arab as a threat and repeated that image for decades, it helped shape how millions of people understood who Arabs were and what could be done to them.

That is what intentional packaging looks like. It is not loud. It is not announced. It is embedded in process, incentive, and repetition.

And once a people are packaged this way, undoing the damage requires more than good intentions. It requires admitting that the package itself was wrong.

That admission, finally spoken by someone with real power, is what this book is responding to.

Chapter 8

When the Truth Is Said Inside the System

What made that moment with a showbiz professional different was not just what was said. It was who said it and where it was said.

This was not a journalist speculating from the outside or an activist calling out Hollywood from afar. This was a studio head, someone who had real influence, real access, and real responsibility, speaking honestly in a professional setting. He was not trying to protect an image. He was not performing for the public. He was speaking to peers who understood exactly how the industry works.

He did not deny the pattern. He did not pretend it was accidental. He acknowledged that Arabs and Palestinians had been portrayed intentionally in negative ways, and he said plainly that doing so was morally corrupt. He did not wrap it in theory or language meant to soften the point. He said it should not have been done, and it should not continue. That matters more than people realize.

Inside Hollywood, most conversations avoid moral clarity.

People talk about risk, audience reaction, marketability, and brand safety. Very rarely does someone in power say, "What we did was wrong." That kind of statement carries weight precisely because it goes against the culture of deflection and plausible deniability.

The room did not react with surprise because the logic was already understood. People inside the industry know that repeated portrayals shape public feeling. They know that packaging a group as dangerous works. They know that audiences absorb these messages even when no one announces them out loud. What made this moment unusual was that the effect was finally named as unethical, not just effective.

From an insider's point of view, this is where responsibility enters.

When something works in Hollywood, it tends to repeat. The same formulas get recycled. The same character types get approved. The same shortcuts get used. Over time, people stop asking whether those choices are right. They only ask whether they are familiar and profitable. Moral questions fade into the background.

That is how harm becomes routine.

The studio head's admission cut through that routine. It acknowledged that the portrayal of Arabs and Palestinians was not just a creative habit. It was a choice that aligned with political outcomes and expansionist aspirations. It helped make violence and dispossession easier to accept. And once that connection is recognized, continuing the same portrayals becomes a conscious decision, not an innocent one.

As a Hollywood talent agent, I understand how difficult it is to challenge a system from within. Careers depend on staying agreeable. Projects depend on fitting expectations. Speaking plainly about moral failure risks discomfort, resistance, and professional consequences. That is why silence is common and honesty is rare.

This is also why that moment mattered enough to write this book.

Once someone with authority admits that an industry practice was morally corrupt, the burden shifts. You can no longer hide behind ignorance or habit. You can no longer say, "That's just how stories are told." The truth has been spoken inside the system. From that point on, continuing the same behavior becomes a choice.

This chapter is not about celebrating a confession. It is about marking a line.

Before that moment, the manufactured image of the Arab could be defended as tradition, coincidence, or market demand. After that moment, it stands exposed as something else, a repeated practice that caused real harm and served real power.

What happens next is the real test.

Hollywood has the ability to tell different stories. It has the resources, the talent, and the reach. The question is not whether it can change. The question is whether it will, now that the moral cost has been acknowledged openly by people inside the industry.

Hollywood's long-standing complicity helped shape a public mindset in which violence against Arabs became easier to accept across multiple fronts. For decades, Arabs were portrayed as threats, fanatics, or disposable figures, not only in relation to Palestine, but in ways that aligned with and normalized wars against Arab populations in Iraq, Libya, Lebanon, and Syria. These portrayals softened public resistance to invasion, bombardment, occupation, and mass civilian suffering and casualties. Collateral damage became an accepted war norm.

The deaths of countless innocent people, including children and the elderly, and the destruction of entire cities and communities across the Arab world did not occur in a moral vacuum. While Hollywood did not fire weapons or authorize military campaigns, some active and influential figures involved in production, planning, and decision-making bear responsibility for shaping the perceptions that made these wars feel necessary, justified, or inevitable.

When stories consistently strip a people of their humanity, the consequences extend far beyond the screen. Responsibility does not end at the edge of the frame.

This book exists because pretending nothing was said would be dishonest. Because allowing that admission to fade into silence would repeat the same pattern that caused the damage in the first place.

When truth is spoken inside a system and nothing changes, the silence that follows becomes its own kind of decision.

Chapter 9

Why Silence Worked So Well

Hollywood did not need to lie loudly to make this work. Silence did most of the work for it.

Once the Arab was packaged as a threat and repeated enough times, the image no longer needed defending. It stood on its own. Writers inherited it. Producers recognized it. Executives approved it. No one needed to restate the logic because it was already understood. Silence became efficiency.

Inside the industry, silence is often mistaken for neutrality. If no one objects, the assumption is that nothing is wrong. If a portrayal keeps getting approved, people assume it must be acceptable. Over time, this creates a culture where questioning familiar images feels unnecessary or even disruptive.

Repetition made the manufactured image feel safe.

Safe does not mean morally sound. It means predictable. It means unlikely to raise eyebrows in a pitch meeting. It means unlikely to scare investors or confuse audiences.

Hollywood rewards what feels safe, even when what feels safe causes harm.

This is why the same portrayals continued long after people privately recognized the problem.

Many writers and actors knew the image was wrong. Some spoke quietly. Some refused roles. Many stayed silent because silence is often the cost of staying employed. The industry does not require agreement. It rewards compliance. When a system rewards silence, silence becomes normal.

What made this silence powerful is that it was shared.

When no one challenges a portrayal openly, each person assumes someone else has already thought it through. Responsibility dissolves. Harm becomes nobody's fault because it belongs to everyone and no one at the same time. That is how morally questionable practices survive inside large systems.

The manufactured Arab benefited from this dynamic.

Because the image was repeated across decades, it became detached from the people it represented. It became a trope, a shortcut, a narrative tool. Once something is treated as a tool, people stop asking what it does outside the story. They focus only on whether it works inside the frame.

Silence also protected the industry from accountability.

As long as means were not named, outcomes did not need to be confronted. As long as portrayals were discussed as "just entertainment," their real-world impact could be dismissed. This allowed Hollywood to continue benefiting from familiar narratives without owning the consequences.

The silence extended beyond film sets and studios. It carried into interviews, award ceremonies, and public conversations. People spoke about diversity and representation in general terms while avoiding specific patterns that were uncomfortable to name. Arabs and Muslims were rarely at the center of those conversations. Their absence made silence easier.

This silence did not require malice. It required convenience.

Breaking silence inside a system like Hollywood is costly. It risks reputations. It risks access. It risks being labeled difficult or political. Many people calculate those risks and decide to stay quiet, even when they know something is wrong. That calculation happens every day in creative industries.

That is why the moment described earlier mattered so much. When someone with power broke the silence and named the practice as morally corrupt, it disrupted the system's most effective defense. Silence only works until someone speaks plainly.

Once silence is broken, repetition looks different. Familiar images no longer feel neutral. They feel intentional. At that point, continuing the same portrayals is no longer passive. It becomes a choice made with awareness.

This chapter is not about condemning everyone who stayed silent. It is about understanding how silence operates as protection. When silence becomes routine, injustice does not need to argue for itself. It simply continues.

Hollywood did not sustain the manufactured image of the Arab through loud declarations. It sustained it by letting the same portrayals pass without challenge for decades. That is why the damage lasted so long.

And that is why speaking now matters more than staying silent or speaking carefully.

Chapter 10

What Changes Once the Truth Is Known

Once something is named honestly inside a system, the system changes, whether it admits it or not.

For decades, Hollywood could claim ignorance. Executives could say stereotypes were accidental. Writers could say they were following tradition. Studios could say they were responding to audience demand. Those explanations only work when no one inside the room says otherwise.

That protection is gone now.

When a studio head openly acknowledges that Arabs and Muslims were intentionally portrayed in negative ways and calls that practice morally corrupt, the industry crosses a line. From that moment forward, repetition is no longer habit. It is choice. Silence is no longer neutral. It is consent.

Hollywood understands accountability better than it admits. When a portrayal is challenged publicly, studios adjust quickly. When a character type becomes unacceptable, it disappears almost overnight. The industry knows how to change when it wants to. That is why the question is no longer about ability. It is about willingness.

What does change look like in real terms.

It means writers stop relying on the manufactured Arab as a shortcut for danger. It means executives stop approving scripts that reduce entire cultures to threats. It means casting decisions reflect humanity instead of stereotype. It means stories slow down long enough to show Arab and Muslim lives as ordinary, complex, and worthy of attention.

Change also means accountability for the past.

Acknowledging harm does not require self-destruction. It requires honesty. It requires admitting that certain portrayals were wrong, not because they offended sensibilities, but because they contributed to real-world outcomes. The industry must recognize that stories helped shape public tolerance for war, occupation, and mass civilian suffering.

This does not mean Hollywood caused every conflict in the Arab world. It means Hollywood helped create an emotional climate where those conflicts could be sold, justified, and sustained with limited resistance. That is a serious responsibility, whether or not it was ever spoken aloud before.

The hardest part of change is not technical. It is moral.

Hollywood often prides itself on being progressive, courageous, and socially aware. That self-image must now confront a harder truth. An industry that claims to champion justice cannot continue reproducing images that strip humanity from entire peoples. The contradiction is no longer invisible.

This is why this moment matters.

Once the truth is known inside the system, every future decision carries weight. Every script approval, every casting choice, every familiar villain packaged as "just a story" becomes a test. The industry can either continue hiding behind tradition or accept responsibility for the influence it wields.

This book is not written to blame Hollywood. It is written to remove its excuses of correction the intentional injustice carried against an entire population.

The manufactured Arab was not an accident. It was built, repeated, and protected. Now that this has been acknowledged openly by those inside the industry, continuing the same portrayals would be an active moral failure.

What happens next will determine whether Hollywood is capable of more than self-congratulation. It will determine whether an industry built on storytelling can finally tell the truth about its own role in shaping the world.

Chapter 11

A Choice, not a Legacy

Hollywood likes to speak about legacy as if it is something that forms on its own, something that appears later and can be admired from a distance. In reality, legacy is nothing more than the sum of repeated choices. When an image appears again and again for decades, it is no longer tradition or coincidence. It becomes responsibility.

The manufactured Arab did not survive in Hollywood because it was accurate. It survived because it was useful.

Inside the industry, usefulness matters. A packaged image saves time. It tells the audience who to fear without explanation. It signals danger instantly. It avoids slowing the story down with context, history, or complexity. In a business driven by speed, familiarity, and predictability, this kind of shortcut is rewarded.

That reward system shaped behavior.

Writers learned early that certain portrayals were easy to sell. Executives learned that audiences would not push back. Studios learned that these images did not threaten box office returns. Over time, the manufactured Arab became a safe choice. And in Hollywood, "safe" often matters more than "right."

This safety was never neutral.

Every time an Arab or Muslim character appeared primarily as a threat, something else disappeared. Ordinary life disappeared. Complexity disappeared. The possibility that the audience might identify, empathize, or hesitate disappeared. The image did its job quickly and efficiently. The story moved on. That efficiency came at a cost that was not paid by Hollywood.

When people are repeatedly portrayed as dangerous or disposable, the audience does not need to be convinced to support harm against them. The audience only needs to be comfortable with it. Comfort is easier to manufacture than hatred, and far more effective.

Hollywood did not invent fear of Arabs and Muslims, but it standardized it. It packaged it. It made it recognizable and repeatable. It taught audiences what to expect and how to feel without ever saying so directly. Over time, this packaging shaped instinct rather than opinion.

That is how manufacturing works.

Once an image becomes familiar, it no longer feels like a choice. It feels like reality. New generations of writers and executives inherit it without asking who built it or why. They repeat it because it already exists. They approve it because it does not raise alarms. Responsibility dissolves into routine. But routine does not erase accountability.

The truth is that Hollywood knows how to change when it decides something is no longer acceptable. The industry has done this before. When certain portrayals became publicly uncomfortable, they were abandoned quickly. Characters disappeared. Language shifted. Standards were rewritten. The speed of those changes proves that inertia is not the real obstacle. Willingness is.

That is why the moment described earlier matters so much.

When a studio head openly acknowledges that the intentional portrayal of Arabs and Palestinians was morally corrupt, the industry loses its final shield. From that moment on, repeating the same images is no longer passive. It is deliberate. It is a choice made with knowledge of the harm caused.

This is where legacy becomes irrelevant.

Legacy allows people to look backward and curate a story about themselves. Choice forces people to look forward and decide what they will continue to do. Hollywood can no longer claim that the manufactured Arab is simply inherited tradition. It has been named as wrong by those inside the system. Continuing it now would mean accepting the damage as acceptable collateral.

That acceptance is a moral decision.

Refocusing Hollywood storytelling does not require censorship or propaganda. It requires discipline. It requires refusing the shortcut. It requires allowing Arab and Muslim characters to exist as ordinary people, with lives that are not defined solely by conflict or violence. It requires telling stories that do not rely on fear as their primary engine.

This is not about making every story "positive." It is about making stories honest and truthful.

Honesty includes showing complexity, contradiction, and humanity. It includes allowing Arab characters to be flawed without being disposable, dangerous without being generic, and human without explanation. That kind of storytelling is harder. It demands attention. It demands care. But Hollywood has never lacked talent. It has lacked restraint.

What stands in the way is not ability. It is habit.

Habits persist because they are comfortable. They allow people to work without questioning their impact. They allow an industry to congratulate itself for progress in some areas while avoiding uncomfortable accountability in others. The manufactured Arab sits squarely in that avoided space.

In this chapter I am calling for honesty about what has already happened. Stories helped shape how millions of people understood Arabs and Muslims. That understanding shaped what those audiences tolerated when wars were sold, cruel occupations continued, and civilian suffering was minimized. That influence cannot be undone retroactively. But it can be stopped.

Every decision going forward matters. Every script that relies on the old package matters. Every executive approval matters. Every casting choice matters. These are not abstract questions anymore. They are concrete choices made by people who know better.

Hollywood's future will not be defined by what it says about itself, but by what it stops doing when the truth becomes inconvenient. The manufactured Arab was built deliberately, maintained quietly, and protected by silence. Undoing that damage requires the same level of intention.

This is not a question of whether Hollywood wants to be admired. It is a question of whether it is willing to be responsible.

That is the choice that Hollywood has to live with.

Chapter 12

The Cost of Convenience

Hollywood often explains its choices using simple language. Tight schedules. Audience expectations. Market realities. These explanations sound reasonable on their own, and in many cases they are true. But when the same explanation is used for decades to justify the same narrow portrayals of the same people, it stops being practical and starts being revealing.

The manufactured Arab survived because it was convenient.

Convenience in Hollywood means speed. It means a character can be understood instantly without explanation. It means a story can move forward without slowing down to provide context, history, or humanity. In an industry where time is money and familiarity reduces risk, convenience becomes a powerful incentive.

The Arab villain, the Muslim extremist, the angry crowd, these images required no setup. The audience already knew how to feel. Fear did not need to be built. Suspicion did not need to be earned. The character arrived pre-loaded with meaning. That made storytelling easier.

But what made storytelling easier made reality harder.

Every time convenience was chosen over accuracy, something was lost. Arab and Muslim characters were stripped of ordinary traits. They were not allowed to be boring, tender, conflicted, or familiar. They were rarely allowed to exist outside moments of danger or crisis. Over time, this taught audiences that these people did not have lives worth following.

When writers used the same shortcuts again and again, they reduced millions of people to a handful of traits. Accent became threat. Clothing became suspicion. Geography became chaos. This flattening did not happen because Hollywood lacked imagination. It happened because imagination was directed elsewhere.

Scripts that relied on familiar images moved faster through development. Scripts that complicated those images raised questions. Questions slow things down. Slowness threatens budgets and timelines. Over time, convenience began to shape not only what was shown, but what was never attempted. This is how exclusion works quietly.

Arab and Muslim stories that focused on daily life, family, work, humor, and love were often labeled risky, niche, or political. Meanwhile, stories that repeated familiar threats were seen as universal, accessible, and safe. The irony is that nothing is more political than deciding whose humanity is shown and whose is omitted.

Convenience allowed Hollywood to avoid responsibility without admitting avoidance.

When challenged, the industry often responded by saying these were just stories, not statements. But stories repeated at scale do not remain isolated. They shape emotional instinct. They teach audiences what feels normal and what feels suspicious. They influence how people interpret real-world events long after the credits roll.

Convenience protected the system from reflection. As long as the manufactured image delivered predictable reactions, there was little incentive to question its impact. The harm it caused did not appear on balance sheets. It appeared in public tolerance for war, occupation, and civilian suffering. That distance made the cost easy to ignore.

Hollywood rarely calculated the long-term effect of convenience. It calculated box office returns, ratings, and reach. Meanwhile, the emotional habits formed by repeated portrayals carried forward into news consumption, political discourse, and public opinion.

Convenience became a form of denial. By relying on the same packaged images, Hollywood avoided confronting its role in shaping perception. It allowed the industry to benefit from influence without owning consequence. The manufactured Arab became a tool that could be used without reflection because its damage was externalized.

The people harmed by these portrayals were not present in pitch meetings. They were not sitting in editing rooms. They were not part of test audiences. Their lives unfolded far from studio lots, in places where the consequences of misrepresentation were felt in real terms.

Convenience also shaped silence. Many individuals inside Hollywood recognized the problem privately. Writers knew the image was tired and harmful. Actors knew the roles were demeaning. Executives knew the patterns were outdated. But convenience discouraged resistance. Challenging familiar portrayals meant risking delays, rejection, or professional friction. Silence was easier.

Over time, convenience trained people not to ask moral questions. When an industry operates this way for long enough, it stops seeing its choices as choices. It sees them as constraints. That illusion is powerful. It allows people to believe they have no alternative when alternatives exist.

The truth is that convenience was never unavoidable. It was selected. Hollywood chose the manufactured Arab because it was faster, safer, and less demanding than telling fuller stories. That choice was made again and again, across decades, until it shaped how millions of people understood Arabs and Muslims.

When an industry chooses ease over accuracy long enough,

it becomes complicit in the harm that follows. The cost of convenience is not theoretical. It is measured in distorted perception, weakened empathy, and a public conditioned to accept violence against people they were never taught to see as fully human.

Convenience saved time. It did not save integrity. And now that this cost is visible, continuing to choose convenience is no longer passive. It is deliberate.

Chapter 13

Who Benefits When Humanity Is Removed

Whenever a group of people is portrayed repeatedly as less than fully human, someone benefits. This is not speculation. It is how power works. When empathy is reduced, resistance weakens. When resistance weakens, decisions that would otherwise face opposition move forward more easily.

Hollywood did not invent this dynamic, but it played a central role in sustaining it.

The manufactured Arab did not exist in isolation. It aligned smoothly with political, military, and economic interests that depended on public tolerance for intervention, war, and long-term instability across the Arab world. When Arabs and Muslims were framed primarily as threats, force against them felt reasonable. When their suffering was familiar rather than shocking, outrage did not last.

This alignment did not require coordination meetings or written directives. It required consistency. Hollywood delivered that consistency.

For decades, audiences were shown the same patterns. Arabs appeared at moments of danger. Muslims were linked to extremism. Arab lands were framed as chaotic, unstable, and violent by nature. Rarely were these places shown as societies with functioning lives disrupted by external forces. Rarely were Arabs shown as people whose loss should interrupt the story.

This framing benefited more than entertainment.

It benefited political narratives that needed public backing for wars in Iraq and Libya, for destruction in Lebanon, for prolonged conflict in Syria, and for ongoing occupation and violence against Palestinians. When audiences are conditioned to associate an entire region with danger, intervention feels preventative rather than aggressive. Civilian casualties feel unfortunate rather than unacceptable.

Hollywood did not cause these wars. But it helped shape the emotional climate in which they were sold. When news coverage followed, it entered a landscape already prepared by entertainment. Audiences were not meeting these regions for the first time. They were meeting them through images they had already learned. The manufactured Arab had already done its work.

This is where benefit becomes visible. Governments benefit when public resistance is low. Military actions benefit when moral scrutiny is brief. Industries tied to conflict benefit when wars feel inevitable. Hollywood, by reinforcing familiar images, helped maintain that environment without ever needing to declare allegiance.

The benefit to Hollywood itself was also real. By aligning with dominant narratives, the industry avoided controversy. It protected access. It maintained relationships. Studios that challenged prevailing images risked being labeled political or risky. Studios that stayed within familiar frames enjoyed smoother production paths. Safety was rewarded.

This is how complicity forms. Complicity does not always look like intention. Often, it looks like alignment without objection. It looks like repeating what works because questioning it feels costly. Over time, alignment becomes normalized, and normalization erases the feeling that a choice is being made.

The people who paid the price for this alignment were not abstract. They were civilians whose deaths did not provoke sustained outrage. Families whose displacement was reported briefly and forgotten. Entire societies reduced to backdrops for fear. Their humanity was removed from the story, and with it, the urgency to protect them.

Hollywood often celebrates itself for challenging power. But in this case, it did the opposite. It mirrored power. It reinforced the assumptions that power needed to operate smoothly. It made violence against certain people easier to

tolerate by making those people harder to recognize.

This chapter is not about assigning blame to a single studio, filmmaker, or executive. It is about naming a system of benefit that operated quietly and effectively. When the same portrayals appear across decades, across genres, and across platforms, they do not survive by accident. They survive because they serve something.

Removing humanity always serves someone.

Now that this alignment has been exposed and acknowledged from within the industry itself, the question becomes unavoidable. Who continues to benefit from repeating the same images, and at what cost?

The answer to that question will determine whether Hollywood remains aligned with power or finally chooses to align with truth.

Chapter 14

What Responsibility Looks Like Now

Responsibility begins at the moment when denial is no longer available. For a long time, Hollywood had room to claim distance. Executives could say portrayals were unintentional. Writers could say they were following genre expectations. Studios could say they were responding to market demand. These explanations worked because the harm was rarely named openly from inside the system itself.

That changed.

Once the intentional nature of these portrayals is acknowledged by people with real power inside the industry, responsibility can no longer be postponed. At that point, continuing the same practices is no longer passive. It is a decision made with awareness of the consequences.

Responsibility does not mean accepting blame for every outcome in the world. It means owning influence.

Hollywood has always understood its influence when it suited its image. It celebrates films that change minds, spark movements, or raise awareness. It claims credit when stories inspire empathy or challenge injustice. That same influence does not disappear when the impact is harmful. Influence

does not turn on and off based on comfort.

Owning influence means recognizing that repeated portrayals shape emotional instinct. They teach audiences what feels normal, what feels dangerous, and what feels unworthy of attention. Over decades, those instincts harden. They do not vanish simply because intentions are later questioned.

So what does responsibility look like now, in real terms.

It looks like refusing to rely on the manufactured Arab as a default. It means stopping the automatic association of Arab and Muslim identity with danger, instability, or violence. It means asking, at every stage of development, whether a character exists as a person or merely as a function designed to provoke fear.

Responsibility looks like slowing down. It means allowing space in stories for ordinary Arab and Muslim life, not as an exception, not as a lesson, but as part of the human landscape. It means showing families, work, disagreement, humor, routine, and contradiction. It means letting Arab characters exist without needing to justify their presence through conflict.

This is not about forcing positivity. It is about ending reduction. Hollywood often resists this kind of change by claiming it threatens creative freedom. In truth, reduction threatens creativity far more. When an industry relies on the same packaged image for decades, it is not exercising imagination. It is avoiding it.

Responsibility also means institutional reflection.

Studios, networks, and production companies must examine how scripts are evaluated, how risks are defined, and how certain portrayals are labeled as "safe" while others are labeled "political." These labels are not neutral. They determine which stories move forward and which are quietly dismissed.

If Arab and Muslim humanity continues to be treated as controversial, while their dehumanization is treated as normal, responsibility has not been met.

There is also responsibility in who is allowed to tell stories.

For years, Arab and Muslim voices were marginalized or filtered through expectations set by others. When those voices were included, they were often asked to explain, defend, or sanitize themselves. Responsibility means making room for creators to tell stories without forcing them into predefined boxes.

This is not charity. It is correction. It's the right thing to do.

Hollywood has corrected itself before. It has abandoned portrayals once considered acceptable when they were recognized as harmful. It has rewritten standards. It has changed language. It has done so not because it lost ability, but because it gained awareness.

That same awareness exists now. What remains is choosing the ethical choice.

Responsibility is not fulfilled by statements, panels, or awards. It is fulfilled by repetition of different choices over time. It is fulfilled when familiar shortcuts are refused even when they are easy. It is fulfilled when silence is replaced by deliberate action.

In this chapter I am not calling on Hollywood to solve every injustice. I am asking those who matter in Hollywood to stop contributing to one they helped sustain.

The manufactured Arab was built through decisions made over decades. Undoing that damage will not happen overnight. But it will never happen at all if the industry continues to treat ethical responsibility as optional.

Ethical responsibility now means this: knowing the harm,

and choosing differently anyway. That is the standard. Anything less is a cowardly retreat.

Chapter 15

A Letter to Hollywood and the Media

This letter is written plainly, without performance, and without the comfort of distance.

I am writing to Hollywood first because I work inside your system. I understand how stories are made, packaged, approved, and repeated. I understand the pressures, the incentives, and the habits that shape what reaches the screen.

I also understand that influence carries responsibility, whether it is acknowledged publicly or not.

For decades, Hollywood helped manufacture a narrow and damaging image of Arabs and Muslims. This image was not accidental. It was built through repetition, convenience, and silence. Arabs were framed as threats. Palestinians were reduced to problems, crowds, or background noise. And Muslims were associated with extremism. Ordinary life was rarely shown. Humanity was often absent.

You now know this. It has been said openly inside your own rooms. Knowing changes responsibility. And requires accountability. Let's start with self-commitment to self-accountability and responsibility.

This letter asks those that matter in Hollywood to stop relying on the same shortcuts and to actively seek better stories. Stories that show Arabs and Muslims as people living full lives, not symbols of danger or conflict. Stories that allow audiences to recognize family, love, work, disagreement, humor, and dignity. This is not about creating a false narrative. It is about correcting a long-standing imbalance that stripped humanity from entire communities.

Hollywood has the talent, the resources, and the reach to do this. The question is no longer whether it can. The question is whether it will.

This letter is also addressed to the media.

CNN, MSNBC, Fox News, The New York Times, and other major outlets that shape public understanding every day. You do not operate in isolation from Hollywood. You report into an environment already shaped by decades of storytelling. But you also reinforce that environment through language, framing, and repetition.

For years, your coverage of the Arab world and Palestine has often reflected the same patterns audiences learned from entertainment. Palestinian deaths were summarized. Israeli narratives were explained. Words like "clashes," "retaliation," and "security" softened the reality of force.

Civilians were reduced to numbers. Stories moved on quickly.

You have the power to slow the story down. You have the power to name who is harmed, how, and repeatedly. You have the power to follow loss over time instead of treating it as a single-day event. Too often, that power was not used.

Good faith matters. Newsrooms are complex. Pressure is real. But systems produce outcomes whether or not every individual intends harm. When the same framing appears across networks and newspapers for years, it shapes public tolerance for violence. That tolerance had consequences.

Wars in Iraq and Libya, destruction in Lebanon, devastation in Syria, and ongoing violence against Palestinians unfolded in a media climate where Arab lives were too often framed as expendable or inevitable losses. You did not cause these events. But your unfair coverage helped determine how long the public stayed outraged and how quickly it moved on.

This letter asks for your courage.

Courage to question familiar language. Courage to resist framing that explains violence before naming its human cost. Courage to show Arab and Muslims life as lived, not only as lost. Courage to follow stories beyond the moment when attention is convenient.

Solidarity does not mean abandoning journalistic standards. It means applying them evenly. It means refusing to strip humanity from one side while amplifying it on another. It means understanding that neutrality in language can still produce moral imbalance.

Hollywood and the media together shaped how millions of people learned who to fear, who to trust, and who to ignore. That influence cannot be undone retroactively. But it can be redirected.

As the Apostle of Compassionate Leadership, I am asking both industries to choose the right compassionate path.

Choose stories that restore humanity rather than erase it. Choose language that clarifies rather than obscures. Choose repetition that builds understanding rather than distance. Choose solidarity with people whose lives were too often reduced to headlines or stereotypes.

This is not a threat. It is not a demand. It is an appeal made with full awareness of the power you hold. You helped manufacture the image. You can help dismantle it.

The choice is no longer hidden. It is yours to make.

Chapter 16

What We Must Also Face

Telling the truth about what was done does not absolve us from looking honestly at ourselves. Dignity includes responsibility. A people without agency are not respected, they are pitied. This chapter is written to refuse pity.

Arabs, Muslims, and Palestinians did not create the systems that portrayed them as disposable or dangerous. They did not control Hollywood studios, Western newsrooms, or global political narratives. But they were not without responsibility of their own, and pretending otherwise weakens the very cause they seek to defend.

Responsibility begins with leadership.

Across the Arab and Muslim worlds, leadership failures have been profound. Corruption, authoritarianism, internal repression, and the silencing of dissent hollowed societies from within. Leaders spoke the language of resistance while protecting their own power. They negotiated behind closed doors while their people paid the price. Palestine was often invoked symbolically, but rarely defended with consistency, strategy, or sacrifice. This fractured leadership diluted moral clarity.

When Arab regimes treated Palestine as a slogan rather than

a responsibility, they trained the world to do the same. When they normalized relations quietly while speaking outrage publicly, they signaled that Palestinian suffering was negotiable. That contradiction weakened solidarity and confused allies.

Responsibility also lies in division. Internal fragmentation among Palestinians and across the Arab world made collective action difficult and, at times, impossible. Political rivalries hardened into permanent fractures. Unity became conditional. Strategy became reactive. These divisions did not justify occupation or violence, but they made resistance less effective and easier to dismiss. A divided people are easier to ignore.

There is also responsibility in silence. Too often, ordinary Arabs and Muslims consumed images and news passively, overwhelmed by scale, fatigued by repetition, or numbed by years of unresolved injustice. Silence became survival. Survival became habit. Habit became disengagement. This did not cause the suffering, but it allowed others to control the narrative unchallenged. Silence has consequences.

There is responsibility in how stories were not told.

While Western media manufactured images, Arab media often failed to counter them effectively. Stories were reactive, emotional, or politicized, rather than steady, human, and sustained. The daily life of Palestinians, their normalcy, their dignity, their complexity, was not consistently documented for the world. The vacuum was filled by others.

Responsibility does not mean matching power. It means using what power exists. Arab and Muslim communities in the West also carry responsibility. Too often, fear of backlash led to self-censorship. Advocacy was framed defensively rather than confidently. Language softened injustice to avoid discomfort. This restraint was understandable, but it allowed others to define the terms of debate.

Agency requires risk. None of this shifts the moral center away from occupation, violence, or ethnic cleansing. Naming internal responsibility does not excuse external crimes. It clarifies the path forward. A people who refuse self-examination remain trapped in reaction. A people who confront their own failures reclaim control of their future.

Responsibility is not an admission of weakness. It is a declaration of strength. The world does not change because injustice exists. It changes when truth is spoken fully,

including the truth that asks something of you, and all of us. Palestinians now more than ever deserve solidarity that is serious, not sentimental. Arabs deserve leadership that acts, not performs. Muslims deserve narratives shaped by courage, not fear. Freedom without responsibility is unsustainable.

Responsibility does not diminish the injustice done to you. It sharpens the demand that it must end. And that is the work that remains.

Chapter 17

Reclaiming the Lens

For Arab and Muslim Americans, participation in media and storytelling is no longer optional. It is necessary.

For generations, others have told stories about you. Often incorrectly. Often unfairly. Sometimes maliciously. The result has been an image that does not reflect who you are, how you live, or what you and your ancestors have contributed to the world. The answer to this is not withdrawal or resentment. The answer is presence and full engagement.

Arab and Muslim Americans must be present at every level of media and storytelling. Not only as actors, but as writers, producers, directors, editors, cinematographers, executives, agents, and decision-makers. Stories are shaped long before a camera turns on. If you are absent from those rooms, your reality will continue to be interpreted by others.

This is a call for your positive and effective action. In this convoluted world, it is your turn to tell us your real and accurate story. We missed the days of Aladin and the magic lamb, thousand and one nights, and many more. Tell us your story.

Your Arab and Muslim civilizations have never been marginal to human progress. They have been central. Long before Hollywood existed, Arab and Muslim scholars were building the intellectual foundations that modern media relies upon today.

The science of optics, which makes cameras possible, was fundamentally advanced by **Ibn al-Haytham** (Alhazen) in the 10th and 11th centuries. His work, *Kitab al-Manazir* (The Book of Optics), established principles of light, vision, reflection, refraction, and the camera obscura. Modern lenses, photography, cinematography, and visual perception are all indebted to his discoveries. This is not symbolic pride. It is documented scientific history.

Mathematics, without which digital media cannot function, was transformed by **Muhammad ibn Musa al-Khwarizmi**, whose work introduced algebra and algorithms. The very word "algorithm" comes from the Latinized form of his name. Every edit, render, compression, and digital process in modern media depends on mathematical systems he helped pioneer.

Medicine, which informs how stories of life, death, trauma, and healing are portrayed, was shaped by scholars like **Ibn Sina** (Avicenna). His *Canon of Medicine* was a standard medical text in Europe for centuries. Hospitals, clinical ethics, and systematic diagnosis were refined in the Muslim world long before becoming Western norms.

Astronomy and navigation, essential to humanity's understanding of space, time, and exploration, were advanced by scholars such as **Al-Battani** and **Al-Zarqali**, whose work influenced later European astronomers, including Copernicus.

Architecture, engineering, chemistry, music theory, and philosophy all carry the imprint of Arab and Muslim thought. These are not ancient footnotes. They are living foundations.

You as descendants of these civilizations are often portrayed as disconnected from progress, hostile to modernity, or incapable of contributing positively to society. This contradiction exists not because of truth, but because of intentional and calculated false repetition and storytelling. When an image is repeated long enough, it becomes familiar. Familiarity is mistaken for reality.

Arab and Muslim Americans especially have a responsibility, not just to themselves, but to the broader society, to interrupt this cycle. That responsibility does not mean defending identity at every turn. It means living openly, working excellently, and telling stories that reflect ordinary humanity. Stories of families, work, love, conflict, humor, failure, generosity, and growth.

Hollywood does not need idealized characters. It needs real ones.

Participation also requires courage. Entering industries that have historically excluded or misrepresented you is not easy. But absence has a cost. Silence allows others to define you. Presence allows you to define yourself.

Arab and Muslim Americans should not wait for permission to belong in media. The tools of storytelling were never foreign to you. The lens itself carries your intellectual fingerprints. The mathematics that drives digital platforms carries the names of your ancestors. Not American names, not Japanese, Not European, and not Chinese, YOUR ancestors' names. The ethics of inquiry and knowledge transmission were central to your traditions.

This is not only about reclaiming the glory of your hidden past. It is about restoring balance. And make Hollywood tell the truth.

The future of storytelling will not be shaped by those who shout the loudest, but by those who show up consistently, work competently, and tell the truth without apology or hostility. Arab and Muslim Americans belong in those spaces, not as exceptions, but as contributors.

The camera is not neutral. It reflects who stands behind it.

I am calling on you. It is time to stand there and tell us your own true beautiful story.

Chapter 18

Have You Ever Really Met an Arab or a Muslim?

Before you answer too quickly, pause.

Not the one on television.

Not the one in a headline.

Not the character written into a script or reduced to a talking point.

I mean, have you ever really met an Arab or a Muslim?

I do not mean shared a seat on a plane or stood in the same grocery line. I mean sat long enough to listen without judgment. Long enough to notice how they speak about their parents. Long enough to see how they treat elders, children, neighbors, even strangers. Long enough to witness what guides them when no one is watching.

Most people answer yes. And most people are wrong.

What they have met is an image that has been rehearsed for them. An identity manufactured through repetition. A character shaped by fear, trimmed of humanity, and

presented as fact. The Manufactured Arab. The Manufactured Muslim.

The real Arab is quieter than the stereotype. Not weak, but measured. Raised with the understanding that dignity is not loud, that honor is carried in restraint. From childhood, respect for elders is not optional, it is instinct. An aging parent is not a burden to be managed, but a living history to be protected. Care for the elderly is not outsourced to institutions, it is absorbed into daily life, into homes, into schedules, into sacrifice. This is not nostalgia. This is a real practice.

The real Muslim is not driven by rage but by discipline. Five daily pauses that interrupt ambition, ego, and chaos, reminding the self that power is temporary and accountability is permanent. Prayer is not performance. It is recalibration. It teaches patience in a world addicted to urgency. It teaches humility in cultures obsessed with self-importance.

Contrary to the narrative, obedience to commandments does not produce blind followers. It produces people who understand limits. Limits on desire. Limits on greed. Limits on harm. The commandments do not erase individuality. They protect it from excess.

The real Arab household teaches generosity before it teaches success. A guest is never rushed. As a matter of fact, it was the Palestinians Arabs who welcomed the refugee Jews who traveled to Palestine after Hitler committed his atrocities against them during the Holocaust. Food is shared even when it is scarce. Hospitality is not strategy, it is identity. One is taught early that how you treat those who enter your home defines who you are, regardless of their faith, their politics, or their language.

Respect for other religions is not a modern adaptation. It is ancestral memory. Muslims are taught that faith cannot be forced, that belief without choice is meaningless. Arab history is filled with shared spaces, churches beside mosques, synagogues protected under Islamic rule, scholars of different faiths studying side by side. These truths do not circulate in the Western world because they disrupt the manufactured image that was created to serve a purposeful goal.

The tragedy is not that the world misunderstands Arabs and Muslims. The tragedy is that it stopped trying to understand them at all.

Despite everything, they remain. Raising families. Caring for elders. Holding faith without hatred. Carrying memory without revenge. That is who they are when the noise fades.

Chapter 19

What the World Uses but Refuses to Name

Every modern city carries Arab and Muslim fingerprints. They are in the hospitals, the universities, the libraries, the laboratories. They are embedded so deeply into Western civilization that removing them would collapse entire systems. And yet, their names are intentionally omitted and now are missing.

This omission was not accidental.

Long before Europe awakened from intellectual stagnation, Arab and Muslim scholars were observing, measuring, recording, and questioning. They built systems where none existed. They preserved knowledge when others burned it. They did not merely translate ancient texts, they corrected them, developed them, expanded them, tested them, and challenged their conclusions.

Medicine moved forward because Muslim physicians

treated the body as a system rather than a superstition. Hospitals as we know them, with wards, records, training, and ethics, did not appear out of nowhere. They were developed, refined, and practiced centuries earlier in Arab cities that valued healing as a moral obligation.

Mathematics did not evolve in isolation. Algebra was not discovered by accident. It was developed to solve real problems, inheritance, commerce, architecture. The numbers that now define global finance arrived through Arab scholarship. Even the word itself remains, stripped of its origin but not its function.

Astronomy advanced because Muslim scholars mapped the skies with precision, not mythology. Navigation became possible across oceans because Arab knowledge of stars, instruments, and mathematics guided ships long before European exploration claimed the seas.

Philosophy survived because Arab thinkers protected it when it was considered dangerous elsewhere. They debated reason and faith not as enemies but as partners. Their writings reentered Europe under different names, cleansed of their origins, presented as rediscovered wisdom rather than inherited brilliance.

What followed was not collaboration but erasure.

As Western civilization advanced, it adopted these Arab and Muslims discoveries, refined them, expanded them, and then quietly reassigned ownership. The source became inconvenient. Acknowledgment would disrupt the narrative of solitary Western genius. So the Arab and Muslim contribution was minimized, footnoted, or removed entirely.

Today, students learn outcomes without origins. Systems without stories. Progress without context. The manufactured version of history allows admiration without accountability.

But, the truth remains stubborn.

The West did not rise alone. It rose on borrowed shoulders. And those shoulders belonged, in large part, to Arab and Muslim minds whose names deserve to be spoken without discomfort.

This book does not ask for gratitude. It asks for honesty. Because civilizations do not advance by pretending they invented everything. They advance by acknowledging who helped them become what they are.

And perhaps the most uncomfortable truth is this: The people of the manufactured Arab who were intentionally and falsely portrayed as backward were once guiding the world forward.

Chapter 20

What Remains When the Screen Goes Dark

When the screen goes dark, what remains is not the story. It is the effect of the story. For decades, images traveled farther and faster than facts. They entered living rooms, classrooms, and conversations. They shaped instinct before thought. They taught millions of people who felt familiar and who felt distant, whose suffering demanded attention and whose could be processed quickly and forgotten.

That work did not disappear when the credits rolled.

The manufactured Arab was not simply a character type. It was a lesson taught quietly over time. It told audiences what to fear, what to dismiss, and what to accept as inevitable. It helped normalize wars far away, civilian deaths explained away, and entire populations reduced to background noise. It did this not through outrage, but through familiarity.

In this book I do not suggest that Hollywood or the media alone caused the violence that followed. Violence has many authors. But culture prepares the ground on which violence is justified, tolerated, or ignored. In that sense, storytelling carries moral weight whether it claims it or not.

What remains now is responsibility.

Responsibility does not belong only to executives, writers, producers, or editors. It belongs to systems that reward repetition without reflection. It belongs to industries that benefit from influence while denying consequences. It belongs to anyone who knows the damage has been done and chooses comfort over correction.

As we end the journey of this book, I am asking for your awareness and action. Awareness that stories shape what people tolerate. Action that refuses to repeat what has already caused harm.

There are other stories to tell. They have always existed. Stories of Arab, Palestinians and Muslim life that include love, disagreement, failure, humor, work, family, and dignity. Stories that do not require violence to justify their presence. Stories that allow audiences to recognize themselves in people they were once taught to see as distant. Choosing those stories is not charity. It is the right thing to do.

This book ends without resolution because resolution belongs to the future. What happens next will not be decided by words on these pages, but by choices made after they are read. Choices made in pitch meetings. Choices made in newsrooms. Choices made quietly, when no one is watching.

The manufactured image was built slowly, deliberately, and repeatedly. It will only be undone the same way.

What remains is the question that cannot be avoided anymore. Now that the truth is known, what will you choose to show? What will you choose to watch? And what will you choose to believe?

References

Recommended Readings

Al-Battānī. (1996). On the science of the stars (C. Burnett, Trans.). Variorum.

Al-Khalili, J. (2011). The house of wisdom: How Arabic science saved ancient knowledge and gave us the Renaissance. Penguin Press.

Al-Khalili, J. (2011). Pathfinders: The golden age of Arabic science. Penguin Books.

Al-Khwarizmi, M. ibn M. (2009). The algebra of Mohammed ben Musa (F. Rosen, Trans.). Forgotten Books.

Al-Zarqali. (1983). Almanac of Azarquiel (E. S. Kennedy, Ed.). University of Pennsylvania Press.

Alsultany, E. (2012). Arabs and Muslims in the media: Race and representation after 9/11. New York University Press.

Amnesty International. (2022). Israel's apartheid against Palestinians: Cruel system of domination and crime against humanity. Amnesty International.

Boggs, C., & Pollard, T. (2006). Hollywood and the spectacle of terrorism. New Political Science, 28(3), 335–351. https://doi.org/10.1080/07393140600872288

Bulliet, R. W. (2004). The case for Islamo-Christian civilization. Columbia University Press.

Dallal, A. (2010). Islam, science, and the challenge of history. Yale University Press.

El-Hibri, T. (2010). Parable and politics in early Islamic history: The Rashidun caliphs. Columbia University Press.

Fakhry, M. (2004). A history of Islamic philosophy (3rd ed.). Columbia University Press.

Gutas, D. (1998). Greek thought, Arabic culture: The Graeco-Arabic translation movement in Baghdad and early Abbasid society. Routledge.

Hallaq, W. B. (2009). An introduction to Islamic law. Cambridge University Press.

Herman, E. S., & Chomsky, N. (1988). Manufacturing consent: The political economy of the mass media. Pantheon Books.

Hodgson, M. G. S. (1974). The venture of Islam: Conscience and history in a world civilization (Vols. 1–3). University of Chicago Press.

Hourani, A. (1991). A history of the Arab peoples. Harvard University Press.

Human Rights Watch. (2021). A threshold crossed: Israeli authorities and the crimes of apartheid and persecution. Human Rights Watch.

Huff, T. E. (2003). The rise of early modern science: Islam, China, and the West. Cambridge University Press.

Ibn al-Haytham. (1989). The optics of Ibn al-Haytham (A. I. Sabra, Trans.). Warburg Institute.

Ibn Sina. (1999). The canon of medicine (L. Bakhtiar, Trans.). Great Books of the Islamic World. (Original work written ca. 11th century)

Kellner, D. (2010). Cinema wars: Hollywood film and politics in the Bush–Cheney era. Wiley-Blackwell.

Lindberg, D. C. (1976). Theories of vision from Al-Kindi to Kepler. University of Chicago Press.

Makdisi, G. (1981). The rise of colleges: Institutions of learning in Islam and the West. Edinburgh University Press.

Nasr, S. H. (1993). An introduction to Islamic cosmological doctrines. State University of New York Press.

Philo, G., & Berry, M. (2011). More bad news from Israel. Pluto Press.

Philo, G., Berry, M., & Schlesinger, P. (2013). Bad news from Israel (Updated ed.). Pluto Press.

Sabra, A. I. (1987). Ibn al-Haytham. In C. C. Gillispie (Ed.), Dictionary of scientific biography (Vol. 6, pp. 189–210). Charles Scribner's Sons.

Said, E. W. (1978). Orientalism. Pantheon Books.

Said, E. W. (1997). Covering Islam: How the media and the experts determine how we see the rest of the world (Rev. ed.). Vintage Books.

Saliba, G. (2007). Islamic science and the making of the European Renaissance. MIT Press.

Shaheen, J. G. (2001). Reel bad Arabs: How Hollywood vilifies a people. Olive Branch Press.

Shaheen, J. G. (2008). Guilty: Hollywood's verdict on Arabs after 9/11. Olive Branch Press.

Shatzmiller, M. (1994). Labour in the medieval Islamic world. Brill.

Touati, H. (2010). Islam and travel in the Middle Ages. University of Chicago Press.

Turner, H. R. (1995). Science in medieval Islam: An illustrated introduction. University of Texas Press.

UN Human Rights Council. (2024). Report of the Independent International Commission of Inquiry on the Occupied Palestinian Territory, including East Jerusalem, and Israel. United Nations.

About Dr. Abraham Khoureis, Ph.D.

DR. ABRAHAM KHOUREIS, PH.D., is a Hollywood talent agent, prolific author, and multi-talented thought leader whose work examines storytelling, power, ethics, and human dignity. As an industry insider, he has spent years working within Hollywood's creative and professional circles, gaining firsthand insight into how narratives are developed, approved, and distributed long before they reach the public.

He is the author of **HOLLYWOOD DREAM: How to Make It in Tinseltown**, a practical and candid guide to navigating the entertainment industry, along with numerous works focused on leadership, media influence, and social responsibility. He is widely known as the *Apostle of Compassionate Leadership.* Dr. Khoureis blends real-world experience with thoughtful analysis, challenging systems without hostility and encouraging accountability grounded in conscience and clarity.

Moreover, Dr. Khoureis developed the Disability Learning Attainment Model, a framework designed to empower individuals with disabilities through inclusive education, skill-building, and leadership development. His work champions and empowers inclusivity, accessibility, and ethical practices in both education and leadership. He has been published on *Forbes.com,*

Newsweek.com, and the distinguished *Leader to Leader Journal*. He was recognized as LinkedIn's Top Leadership and Management Voice, and Thinkers360's Top 50 Voices.

Dr. Abraham's contributions extend to his writings, professional development initiatives, and thought leadership, making him a respected emerging leader in the fields of compassionate leadership, entertainment, organizational behavior, and human resources development.

In *The Manufactured Arab*, he brings his industry knowledge and scholarly perspective together to examine representation, perception, and the human consequences of false storytelling, while calling for greater participation and truth in media and cultural production.

Easily accessible at:

DrAbeKhoureis.com – DrAbeBooks.com

AuthorAbeKhoureis.com

Social Media: @DrAbeKhoureis

On Amazon.com, search for Dr. Abraham Khoureis

Other Books by Dr. Abraham Khoureis, Ph.D.

The Balance In Between: Finding the Balance Between Emotional Intelligence and Emotional Stupidity. ISBN: 979-8-9895211-2-8

Hollywood Dream: How To Make It In Tinseltown ISBN: 979-8-9895211-7-3

Decoding Microaggressions for Leaders and Beyond: Understanding Microaggressions Face-to-Face. ISBN: 979-8-9895211-4-2

Reasonable Accommodation: Empowering Inclusion. ISBN: 979-8-9895211-3-5

SELF: Introducing The Self Rotating Model.
ISBN: 979-8-9895211-5-9

The Compassionate Leadership Model and Pyramid. ISBN: 979-8-9895211-0-4

Revealing The Seven Secrets to Exceptional Mentorship. ISBN: 979-8-9895211-8-0

For his latest published books:

Visit Amazon.com, search for Dr. Abraham Khoureis

www.ingramcontent.com/pod-product-compliance
Lightning Source LLC
LaVergne TN
LVHW091010080826
845145LV00003B/1213

* 9 7 8 1 9 6 6 8 3 7 4 8 0 *